HERCULES
AND OTHER
GREEK MYTHS

by Mark Gave
illustrated by Jerry Harston

GT
PUBLISHING
NEW YORK

Aphrodite *goddess of love*
Athena *goddess of wisdom*
Dionysus *god of wine*
Eris *goddess of discord*

Hera *queen of the gods*
Hercules *the half-human son of Zeus*
Zeus *king of the gods*

L ong, long ago the Greeks worshipped many gods whom they believed lived on a mountain called Mount Olympus. There was a god for love, a god for art and a god for war. There were gods for rivers, rocks, and trees—in fact, there were gods for everything in the world. Stories about the gods interacting with the people they ruled are called myths.

Hercules was the strongest man on earth, but that didn't make his life easy. The King of Mycenae forced him to perform twelve life-threatening tasks, which are known as the twelve labors of Hercules.

First, Hercules was sentenced to kill the lion of Nemea, a fierce magical beast whose skin no weapon could pierce. After a fearsome battle, Hercules caught the lion in his bare hands and squeezed the life out of it.

Then Hercules had to conquer the Hydra, a monster with nine snaky heads and breath so terrible that it killed anyone who smelled it. Holding his breath, Hercules swung his club at the Hydra, only to find that each time he cut off a head, two grew back in its place. Finally, he torched them off and was victorious.

Hercules' next mission was to clean King Augeas' stable which had not been cleaned in over thirty years and was teeming with cattle and vermin. Hercules made enormous holes in the stable wall with his club, and then changed the course of two rivers so they would flow through the stable and sweep away the mess.

After completing eleven extremely difficult labors, Hercules was faced with the most dangerous task of all: to capture Cerberus, the three-headed dog that guarded the gates of the underworld. When Hercules brought the beast back to the king, the king was so terrified that he begged Hercules to take Cerberus back. "Only if you promise that my labors are done," warned Hercules.

The king agreed. Hercules was free to marry the beautiful Deianira and roam the land performing other heroic deeds. At the end of his life on earth he was carried up to Mount Olympus where he joined the gods—the only mortal ever to do so.

His legend will be remembered always. Do you know why? The constellation Hercules shines in the night sky.

There was once a kind but foolish king named Midas. To reward Midas for his kindness, the god Dionysus granted him a wish. Without thinking, Midas blurted out, "I wish that whatever I touch shall turn to gold!"

Delighted with his new power, Midas danced through his palace, turning everything into bright, shiny gold.

But before long Midas realized that his new gift was not as wonderful as he had thought. When he sat down to eat, all the food and drink turned into gold the second he touched it.

"What am I to do?" he cried in despair. "Even the richest man on earth has to eat and drink!"

The king's cries reached the ears of his beloved daughter, who came running to comfort him. Before Midas could stop her, she flung her arms around him—and she instantly turned into a shimmering golden statue.

When Midas saw what he had done, he was horrified. "Oh, my dear daughter! I'd rather see your face smiling up at me than have all the gold in the world."

Dionysus had been watching and took pity on the king. He undid the wish, and everything in the palace went back to the way it had been.

Midas was grateful to have his daughter back—but sometimes he sure did miss that gold!

The goddess Eris loved to stir up trouble. One day she saw the gods of Olympus enjoying themselves at a wedding feast to which she had not been invited. Throwing a beautiful golden apple among them, she shouted, "This is for the fairest of the fair."

At once, Hera, Aphrodite, and Athena began to fight over the apple. Each of the three goddesses believed herself to be the most beautiful.

Zeus knew something had to be done. So he selected a young human named Paris to judge who should get the apple.

"Give it to me," Hera told Paris, "and I shall give you power."

"Give it to me," said Athena, "and I shall give you wisdom."

"Give it to me," Aphrodite coaxed, "and I shall give you the most beautiful woman on earth."

Beauty was more important to Paris than power or wisdom. So he gave the apple to Aphrodite, and in return she led him to Helen, Queen of Sparta, whose beauty was legendary. Helen was already married to the Greek King Menelaus, but that didn't stop Paris. He sailed with her across the sea to his home in Troy.

It wasn't long before King Menelaus led an army against Troy to take his wife Helen back. The Trojans refused to let her go, and a war broke out that lasted ten years. The king's army couldn't break through the high, strong wall around Troy, and the Trojans couldn't drive the Greeks back to their ships.

Suddenly, after years at war, the Trojans looked over their wall and realized that the Greek army had disappeared. The only thing left was a huge wooden horse. Assuming that their enemy had given up and sailed away, leaving the horse as a gift, the Trojans brought the giant horse into the city and began to celebrate. They had no idea that the horse was filled with Greek soldiers. In the dead of night the soldiers crept out and opened the city gates to the rest of the army hiding nearby. And before the Trojans knew what had happened, the Greeks entered Troy and destroyed it.

And finally, after ten years of fighting, Helen returned home to Sparta.